HANGING BASKETS

Glorious hanging baskets for year-round interest,
shown in over 110 inspirational photographs

ANDREW MIKOLAJSKI

LORENZ BOOKS

This edition is published by Lorenz Books
an imprint of Anness Publishing Ltd
Blaby Road, Wigston, Leicestershire LE18 4SE
info@anness.com

www.lorenzbooks.com; www.annesspublishing.com

If you like the images in this book and would like to investigate using
them for publishing, promotions or advertising, please visit our website
www.practicalpictures.com for more information.

A CIP catalogue record for this book
is available from the British Library.

Publisher: Joanna Lorenz
Editor: Valerie Ferguson
Photography: Peter Anderson, Jonathan Buckley, Derek Cranch,
John Freeman, Michelle Garrett, Janine Hosegood, Simon McBride,
Marie O'Hara, Debbie Patterson and Polly Wreford
Series Designer: Larraine Shamwana
Designer: Ian Sandom
Production Manager: Steve Lang

PUBLISHER'S NOTE
Although the advice and information in this book are believed to be accurate and
true at the time of going to press, neither the authors nor the publisher can
accept any legal responsibility or liability for any errors or omissions that may
have been made nor for any inaccuracies nor for any loss, harm or injury that
comes about from following instructions or advice in this book.

CONTENTS

Introduction

HANGING BASKETS ADD AN EXTRA DIMENSION TO GARDENING –
POSITIONED JUST ABOVE EYE LEVEL, THEY INVITE YOU TO LIFT YOUR
GAZE SKYWARDS. WHETHER YOU PLANT FOR SUBTLETY OR GO FOR A
RIOT OF COLOUR, THEY MAKE FOR INSTANT APPEAL.

ENJOYING HANGING BASKETS

Hanging baskets are a form of gardening that is available to everyone, even those who have no garden. Fixed to house walls, they are an extension to the home, bringing pleasure every time you walk through the door. They are democratic: delightfully framing the doorway of an elegant town house, they are equally at home at the entrance to a country cottage. They can be fixed near a kitchen window – if you want to grow herbs, for instance. They can also be suspended on either side of a patio door and enjoyed from inside when it is too wet or cold to venture outdoors. They are also the ideal way for a city-dweller to experience something of the thrill of growing things.

DECIDING WHAT YOU WANT

A wealth of plants can be grown in baskets, not just the traditional lobelias, pelargoniums and fuchsias, splendid though these are. While they are generally associated with summer, you can plant baskets for spring, autumn or even winter interest, because many plants flower at these cooler times of year, even if the choice may not be as great.

Hanging baskets are also extremely versatile as they can be enjoyed in many ways. Most people think of them as vehicles for vibrant summer flowers, but they can be used not just for flower plantings, but also for plants with variegated or coloured leaves, herbs, and even fruit and vegetables. In a conservatory (sunroom), use them for trailing rainforest plants, such as cacti, ferns and orchids.

Above: *Extend a border vertically by using the same colours in an eye-level arrangement of plants.*

MAKING AN IMPACT

As with many other types of container, hanging baskets offer boundless opportunities to experiment. You can try out all kinds of colour combinations and be as subtle as you like or as ritzy as you dare. You can use an arbitrary mix of flowers that will certainly be cheerful if not elegant or you can adopt a more sophisticated approach and plan the effect from the outset. Hot vibrant colours, such as red, orange and yellow, will always make an impact, while soft blues, pinks, cream and white are more soothing. Purples are ambivalent, adding drama to an already brilliant planting but sounding deeper notes in a gentler pastel scheme.

Above: This charming planting uses polyanthus, pansies and dwarf narcissi to brighten a gloomy corner in spring.

Below: This subtle arrangement makes effective use of the silky-textured, silver-leaved Helichrysum petiolare.

DECIDING ON STYLE

Some of the best hanging baskets are to be found in municipal schemes and adorning the streets of towns, where they are often paid for by the shopkeeper. The baskets are usually planted for summer interest and often contain bright, eye-catching colours. You can, of course, copy these at home, but there is no reason you cannot add a personal touch. An informal mixture of plants suits a cottage garden, for instance, whereas an elegant, white-painted, stuccoed house needs a more tightly controlled look, perhaps involving no more than two colours. If you favour a very minimalist style, try a few hanging rat's-tail cacti with perhaps a spiky aloe for height. For a funky look, try using one of the more compact grasses, such as *Festuca glauca*.

INTEREST THROUGH THE YEAR

Hanging baskets are traditionally associated with summer, but they can also be enjoyed at other times of year. Spring baskets, possibly involving some dwarf bulbs, such as daffodils, irises or crocuses, with a few early bedding plants, are always a delight, but it is also possible to enjoy baskets in autumn with a combination of tender perennials – which seem to go on flowering for ever – with the addition of some late-sown annuals. Winter baskets offer less scope, but it is still possible to have some choice of colour. Choose robust, winter-flowering heathers and hardy pansies, and even dainty ivies, whether colourful variegated varieties or plain green, can be surprisingly interesting and attractive.

SUN OR SHADE

Once you have decided where your baskets are to go, the amount of sun or shade the position offers will influence your choice

Above: *This glorious display uses pale pink nemesias to offset the rich purples of the verbenas and pansies.*

Left: Coelogyne velutina *is a robust orchid with trailing flower stems, which, together with the upright leaves, create an unusual effect.*

reason. However, a large basket would be first choice for growing fruit and vegetables, which normally need a good root run to develop properly. Smaller baskets create a daintier effect but perhaps offer less scope for exciting colour combinations.

How to Use This Book

You will find all the information you need for creating successful baskets on the following pages. *Getting Started* deals with such practical matters as choosing a suitable basket, selecting an appropriate potting mix, buying plants, planting the basket and maintaining it. Watering, feeding and dealing with pests and diseases are also covered. The subsequent sections are full of ideas, with *Baskets for All Seasons* illustrating a range of baskets planted for seasonal appeal, whether your taste is for subtle or brilliant or for dramatic foliage effect. Herb, fruit and vegetable baskets are also given due attention. In *Satisfying the Senses* you will find ideas for plants to smell and touch as well as stimulating the eye. Finally, there are some useful lists of seasonal tasks, recommended plants with information on plant type, season of interest, flower colour and cultivation tips, and the common names of plants to help with identification.

of plants. Many of the summer flowers are sun worshippers, but remember that in a very sheltered spot against a warm wall, the heat on a hot summer's day will be intense. Reserve such a favoured spot for real exotics, such as South African osteospermums. Many plants will thrive in shade. Lobelias are shade tolerant, and begonias and busy Lizzies actually prefer it. Fuchsias usually do best if kept out of direct sun.

Size Matters

The size of the basket is an important consideration. Although large baskets are the most spectacular and can house the greatest number of plants, they will take up a lot of space when the plants are mature and will be heavy, particularly when wet. That can be an issue if you need to move the basket for any

Getting Started

ONCE YOU HAVE DECIDED WHAT YOU WANT YOUR HANGING
BASKETS TO PROVIDE, YOU CAN BEGIN TO EXPLORE THE MANY TYPES
THAT ARE AVAILABLE AND DECIDE WHICH BEST SUITS YOUR NEEDS AND
THE STYLE OF PLANTING YOU HAVE IN MIND.

TYPES OF HANGING BASKETS

Hanging baskets come in all shapes
and sizes, and when you come to shop
for one you will be amazed at the
range available. The traditional basket
is half a sphere and is usually made of
plastic-coated wire, with three chains
to hang from. Wrought iron is also
sometimes used, especially for hay
baskets, which are meant to be fixed
directly against a wall. More ornate
antique baskets (and, increasingly,
reproductions of these) can be found,
but decorative as these are, they are

usually less sturdy, so are less suitable
for a very heavy planting. Decide
whether it is the basket itself or the
plants that are in it that will be the
focus of interest.

Some baskets really are baskets and
are made of wicker or bamboo or
some other twiggy material. Many are
beautiful to look at and are perhaps
best with a simple planting. It is not
always possible, or indeed desirable,
to plant through the sides of such containers. Unless they have been treated
with some kind of preservative, they

Above: *Plastic-coated wire baskets.*

Above: *Wrought iron and galvanized wire baskets.*

will be vulnerable to changes in the weather and may dry out and split in hot sun. They may need to be replaced after a few seasons, while a metal basket is virtually indestructible and will last for many more years than those made of wicker or bamboo.

The ideal basket is strong but lightweight. It will be heavy enough once it is full of moist soil and all the plants have reached their optimum size so you do not want to start off with a heavy basket that is going to add substantially to the overall weight.

Some baskets are sold already lined with plastic, but remember to pierce this before use to allow for drainage.

Above: Small hanging baskets often look most effective when a single flower colour is used.

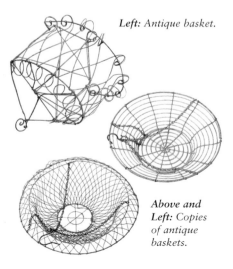

Left: Antique basket.

Above and Left: Copies of antique baskets.

Brackets and Other Fixings

All hanging baskets have to be mounted, and usually some form of wall bracket is required. To determine the size of the bracket, you need to calculate how wide the basket will be once it is planted up and mature, then divide this figure by two. This is the minimum distance it will need to hang from the wall so that the plants can be displayed properly. Look for sturdy brackets that will not buckle under the weight of the basket and that are made from rust-proof material. Hanging baskets can also be suspended from hooks attached to the cross-beam of an archway or pergola or screwed to the ceiling of a conservatory (sunroom).

Above: This antique wicker bird cage is such a thing of beauty that it needs only the simplest planting.

Other Types of Container

Apart from the traditional hemispherical shape, other types of container are available. Your choice will often be determined by the type of plant you wish to grow.

Orchid baskets are shallow, usually square and made of wooden slats. They are designed to allow plant roots to grow through and grip the sides. Orchid potting mix is coarse enough not to slip through the openings. The baskets are usually designed for indoor use and are not robust enough to stand up to the weather. Similar baskets are available for other tropical plants that need air around their roots, such as some ferns and cacti.

Ideas for Improvising

If you like to experiment, keep a sharp eye out for objects that were intended for quite different purposes but that can be used as hanging baskets. Antique bird cages are very beautiful and make a witty statement hanging from the branches of a tree. For a cottage kitchen look, use an old metal colander. These are particularly effective and appropriate for culinary herbs or other edible crops. Look out for them in flea markets and junk shops. Car sales and second-hand stores are also a valuable source of unusual but usable hanging containers.

Above: Slatted baskets are ideal for orchids and other tree-dwelling plants.

Some products, often based on recycled sisal, look remarkably natural. Coir lining is sometimes sold in rolls or ready cut to fit certain sizes of basket. Convenient pressed cardboard liners are pre-formed to fit various sizes of basket.

Remember that once the planting is mature, the liner will be all but invisible, so a material that at first glance looks a little unsympathetic will soon be hidden from view. This is especially the case with summer baskets.

Different Linings

What you line your basket with is a matter of choice. The traditional material is moss, but, like peat, this is not a renewable resource, and many feel that alternatives are preferable.

Above: This unusual edible hanging basket partners dwarf beans with decorative curled parsley. Sage or summer savory would look just as attractive as the parsley.

11

CHOOSING A COMPOST

There are a number of different composts (soil mixes) on the market, some all-purpose, others tailored for specific needs. Loam-less mixtures, which are light, are usually best.

Loam-based compost
is based on soil.
It is high in
nutrients but
also heavy. It
can easily be
lightened by
adding perlite
or vermiculite.

**Lime-free
(ericaceous)
compost**
is specially for-
mulated for those
plants that will
not grow in limey
conditions, such as
many of the heathers
and azaleas.

**All-purpose
compost** is
cheap and light
to handle, but
many are based on
peat, which is not a
renewable resource,
and most gardeners now prefer to
look around for more ecologically
acceptable peat-free alternatives.

Peat-free compost
is also an
all-purpose
compost, but,
for ecological
reasons, is usually
based on a
renewable
resource such
as coir or bark.

**Hanging basket
compost**
is lightweight
and often
contains some
water-retaining
crystals and slow-
release fertilizers, but
it may be peat-based.

Above: If the compost does not already contain water-retaining gel, you can mix some in before planting, pre-soaking if necessary so that it expands with water.

Above: Pelleted fertilizers, which are very easy to use and can feed for a whole season, are a low-maintenance option.

Orchids and cacti need specially formulated, free-draining, proprietary composts. Ordinary composts retain too much moisture and are not suitable for these plants.

WATERING AND FEEDING

Whatever compost you choose, you can cut down on watering by adding water-retaining gels. Some need pre-soaking; others can be added directly to the compost. Most new composts contain some plant food, but this is usually exhausted after 6 weeks. To keep the plants flowering well, you should give a high-potash plant food. Tomato fertilizers are suitable, but you can also buy special hanging basket formulas. Pelleted

fertilizers are easy to handle and feed the plant as they break down in the compost. One application will last for a whole season, but check, as individual products vary.

Liquid feeds are sold either as powders to be dissolved in water, as liquids to be diluted or as ready-mixed products. They are usually watered into the compost as a root drench at intervals, depending on the product. Some can be sprayed directly on to the foliage as a foliar feed, and these are especially good for giving your plants an instant boost if they have suffered a set-back, such as an unexpected cold spell or pest attack – but a certain amount of the product is inevitably lost.

Above: Using the right compost and feeding regularly will ensure that the plants in your hanging baskets flower for longer.

THINKING AHEAD

Hanging baskets have to be planned far in advance. Although it is possible to buy plants in flower for instant impact, this is an expensive option and the flowers are likely to be short-lived if they have been forced out of season. As a general rule, you need to plant up your baskets 6–10 weeks before the main season of interest. Spring-flowering bulbs, for instance, are sold in autumn and winter and should be planted at that time.

BUYING PLANTS

The best advice when buying plants is to go to a reputable garden centre or nursery. Bedding plants are sold in strips, but larger plants such as ivies, pelargoniums and fuchsias are usually potted individually. 'Plugs', basically young plantlets with well-developed root systems, are often sold via mail order by seed merchants; busy Lizzies, fuchsias, pelargoniums and begonias are often marketed this way.

If possible check the plant before purchase to make sure that it is not harbouring any pests or diseases. Bedding plants should have fresh, bright green foliage, with no hint of yellowing, and should be compact, not straggly. Potted plants should have a good root system. If possible, slide the plant from the pot. The roots should fill the pot nicely without being tightly coiled. Select plants that have plenty of healthy buds that are not yet open.

Bulbs are sold when dormant (usually in autumn and winter). Buy them from a reputable garden centre or nursery and look for firm, plump bulbs that show no signs of withering or fungal disease.

Left: Pansies can be relied on to provide a colourful display over a long period. They are available in a wide variety of shades, either singly coloured or in bold combinations such as this bright yellow and maroon pairing.

PLANTING

The aim when planting a hanging basket is to use as many plants as you can. The normal rules of carefully spacing plants to allow them to reach their full potential do not apply.

1 If you are using moss or an equivalent to improve water retention, place a circle of plastic, pierced to allow drainage, at the base of the basket.

2 Line the basket with the chosen liner, making holes in the liner with scissors or a sharp knife, if necessary.

3 Fill the basket about one-third of the way up with the appropriate compost (soil mix), tamping it down lightly with your fingers to remove any air pockets.

4 Push trailing plants through the side of the container, resting the rootballs on the surface of the compost.

5 Add more compost and plant the top of the basket. Angle the plants at the edge slightly so that they will trail outwards and cover the rim of the basket.

HANGING THE BASKET

You need good do-it-yourself skills to fix the brackets to the wall. Hanging baskets are heavy for their size when they are moist and full of mature plants and they can also be blown about in strong winds, so proper fixing is essential for safety. Use rawl plugs and long screws to hold them securely in position.

15

Routine Care

Hanging baskets need a certain amount of regular care and attention if they are going to give the display you want. Don't forget that you are asking the plants to outperform their garden counterparts, and, crammed into the basket, they are competing for water, light and nutrients.

Watering

Even if you added water-retaining gels to the compost (soil mix), you will find that the compost in summer baskets quickly dries out. You will need to water the basket every day, and twice a day during the long hot days of summer. Morning or evening is the best time, because leaves can

Above: An automatic drip feed system can save time and effort and will be useful if you are away on holiday.

scorch if they get wet in the full heat of the sun. You may find that the compost is dry even after a rainy spell as dense leaf coverage makes it difficult for water to reach the compost.

Water with a can, making sure the tip of the spout reaches the compost. If you can lift only a small can, one canful may not be enough.

Watering winter and spring baskets is a matter of judgement. The plants are unlikely to be growing strongly and will need watering only when the compost is dry. Over-wet compost in cold weather can lead to root rot.

Feeding

To keep the plants growing strongly and flowering well you will need to feed them. Unless you added a slow-release fertilizer to the compost, apply a high-potash liquid feed every two to three weeks.

Above: Use a watering can with a spout so that you wet the compost thoroughly.

Above: Pinching out fuchsias and pelargoniums regularly will give a fuller plant with a better shape and more flowers.

Pinching Out

This involves removing the growing tips of young plants to make them bush out and thus produce more flowering stems. Use just your thumb and forefinger to remove the tips. If this is done regularly the plant will have a better, more even shape.

Deadheading

Removing faded flowers not only keeps the baskets looking good, but encourages the plants to produce further flowers rather than expending their energies on seed production. As the flowers begin to go over, either pinch back the stems or trim them off with secateurs (pruners) or scissors. If you want to propagate the plant from seed, to provide plants for the following year, allow a few flowers to go to seed at the end of the season when they can be collected and stored.

Pruning

Few hanging basket plants will need pruning, but you may find that woody-stemmed plants, such as fuchsias, will benefit from a trim if they start to become a bit leggy and overgrown. Trim them back as necessary, cutting just above a leaf joint. Ensure that you use sharp secateurs so that you achieve a clean cut.

Above: Deadheading flowers as they fade will encourage a succession of blooms.

17

PROPAGATION

While most people are happy to buy nursery-grown plants, green-fingered gardeners like to raise their own plants. Many annuals are easily raised from seed, and woody-based perennials can be increased by taking cuttings. Overwintered, these can provide material for baskets the following year.

Growing from Seed

Fill trays or pots with seed compost, firm down lightly, water well and allow to drain. Scatter the seed on the surface and cover with sieved compost to its own depth. (Very fine seed does not need to be covered.) Water in lightly and place in a light position but out of direct sunlight.

Placing the seeds in a heated propagator can speed up germination but is by no means essential. Seed packets carry full information on the requirements of different species. When the seedlings are growing strongly, pot them on individually and grow them on until large enough for use.

Taking Cuttings

A simple, inexpensive way to multiply your stock or provide new plants for the following year's baskets.

1 In late summer to early autumn take cuttings about 10cm (4in) in length from non-flowering sideshoots (remove the flowers if necessary) cutting cleanly just above a leaf joint.

2 Trim the cuttings just below a leaf joint and trim off the lower leaves. Ensure that your knife is sharp and clean so that you do not create a ragged edge which could encourage diseases.

3 As soon as possible after taking the cuttings, insert a few of them up to two-thirds their length in a half-and-half mix of peat (or alternative) and sharp sand or vermiculite. Cover with a plastic bag that does not touch the leaves. Keep the cuttings in a sheltered spot out of direct sunlight. Make sure the compost never dries out but do not overwater, otherwise the cuttings may rot.

4 Pot up the rooted cuttings in standard compost and overwinter them in a frost-free place until ready to plant up in a hanging basket the following year.

PLANTS TO INCREASE BY CUTTINGS

Argyranthemum
Diascia
Felicia
Fuchsia
Helichrysum
Pelargonium
Verbena

USING PESTICIDES

Plants in hanging baskets are usually grown for one season only before they are discarded, which means that they rarely succumb to diseases. They are, however, susceptible to attack by a number of insect pests. Although keeping your plants healthy by feeding and watering them regularly will increase their resistance, you may occasionally find it necessary to use chemicals to keep pests under control.

There are two main types of pesticide. Contact pesticides are sprayed directly on to the pests and are usually instantly effective. Use specific formulations to avoid harming beneficial insects, such as ladybirds (ladybugs), hoverflies and bees. Systemic pesticides are watered into the compost and are absorbed by the plant so that insects that feed on the plant are killed. The effect is not immediate, but this is a good way of dealing with sap-sucking pests, such as aphids.

Aphids

These common pests suck sap from plants and can transmit diseases. Green- and blackfly are most often seen, clustering on young shoots and the undersides of leaves.
Control: Use a systemic pesticide.

Red Spider Mite

The mites, which are barely visible to the naked eye, are prevalent in warm, dry conditions in the garden and under glass. They are often overlooked until the fine webs and mottled leaves are seen.
Control: Pick off and burn infested shoots; mist plants regularly; under glass introduce biological controls.

Vine Weevil Larvae

The fleshy, white grubs are active beneath the compost and are rarely seen. They eat roots, causing plants to collapse. Look out for them when you are re-potting plants because most hanging baskets will be inaccessible to the adult insect.
Control: Use treated compost or water in a specific chemical pesticide.

Whitefly

The tiny white flies are a particular pest in greenhouses and conservatories (sunroom), especially in dry conditions.
Control: Maintain a humid atmosphere; use either systemic or contact pesticides; under glass introduce a biological control (*Incarsia formosa*).

Above: Check for the presence of blackfly on the undersides of leaves.

19

Baskets for All Seasons

ALTHOUGH THEY ARE USUALLY ASSOCIATED WITH SUMMER, HANGING BASKETS CAN BE DESIGNED TO PROVIDE INTEREST THROUGHOUT THE YEAR. IF YOU PLAN CAREFULLY, YOU CAN HAVE FRESH, BRIGHT FOLIAGE AND COLOURFUL FLOWERS SEASON AFTER SEASON.

SPRING BASKETS

This is the season of dwarf bulbs, many of which can be grown with ease in baskets. However, they tend to be stiffly upright. Few flowering plants at this time of year are natural trailers, so to soften the edges of the basket, you will have to rely on the old stalwarts, ivy (*Hedera*) and periwinkle (*Vinca*).

Early dwarf bulbs include the indispensable snowdrops (*Galanthus*) and two irises, *Iris danfordiae* (yellow) and *Iris reticulata* (mostly in shades of blue and purple). Most bulbs need

---

PLANTS AT THEIR BEST IN SPRING

Crocus
Galanthus
Myosotis
Narcissus (dwarf cultivars)
Primula
Vinca minor
Viola

---

good drainage, so remember to choose a light, free-draining compost (soil mix). When they have finished flowering, plant the bulbs out in the garden.

Your hanging baskets can be a last-minute inspiration, if you neglected to plan ahead. Simply dig up clumps from the garden and plant them up.

Planting Partners

Polyanthus (*Primula*), grown from seed sown the previous year, are delightful, low-growing plants with flowers in a range of jewel-like colours. Some have attractive markings in more than one colour. Use them on their own or to contrast with or complement dwarf narcissi, such as 'Tête-à-Tête', 'Jenny' or 'Jumblie'.

Left: A classic spring combination, forget-me-nots, miniature narcissi and pansies always look delightful together.

Above: Dwarf tulips, grape hyacinths and cheeky-faced violas make for a vibrant colour combination.

Easy-to-grow grape hyacinths *(Muscari armenaicum)* are more subtle, with deep purple-blue flowers like miniature bunches of grapes. They go well with the brighter blue of forget-me-nots *(Myosotis)*. Crocuses are also a good bet, especially sturdier cultivars such as 'Snow Bunting' (white) and 'Dutch Yellow' (yellow).

Extending the Display

Most bulbs have brief seasons compared to other plants you might be using at this time of year. To extend the period of interest of the basket, plan for a succession of bulbs – for instance, early crocuses, followed by mid-season daffodils, then late dwarf tulips – and pot them up in containers, one type in each. As the buds of the

earliest bulbs start to show colour, plunge the pot into the centre of the basket. When the flowers have faded, replace the pot with the one holding the later bulbs, and so on.

Planning Ahead

Plant iris bulbs in autumn to winter when they become available in shops and garden centres. Snowdrops are best planted up as growing plants.

Above: Planting bulbs in pots means you can replace them after flowering.

SUMMER BASKETS

No matter how much time and attention you lavish on your hanging baskets at other times of the year, summer is their peak season, as it is for the garden at large. At no other time of year will you have such a wide choice of plant material, offering you a wealth of colour, form and scent. This is the time when all your plans will pay off.

If it is properly cared for, a summer basket will provide pleasure for up to three months of the year, and possibly even longer. At the height of summer, the basket itself and the lining material should be invisible, covered by a mass of flowers.

Different Styles

Plant baskets the way you would plant any other area in your garden. If the cottage garden style appeals to you, use simple plants in a range of colours. Many cottage favourites, such as pinks (*Dianthus*) and nasturtiums, are ideal basket material if you stick to shorter cultivars. For a sophisticated look, team pastels with grey-leaved *Helichrysum petiolare*.

An Airborne Rose Garden

If you have a passion for roses, extend that towards some of the many miniatures and patio roses, which are ideal for containers of all kinds. Many of the so-called ground-cover roses

Above: Fuchsias, petunias and lobelias are the epitome of summer plantings.

Left: Many miniature roses are dainty enough to be grown in a hanging basket.

the place of more familiar fuchsias and pelargoniums. These plants are often sold unnamed in many florists, sometimes out of season. In a mild spell in spring, autumn or even winter, you could use one as a temporary planting. If you want the basket to be permanent, protect the roots from frost in winter – they are more vulnerable than plants in the ground. Remember that, if you are intending to use a rose, you will have to watch out for the attendant

have long, flexible stems, which will trail over the edge of a hanging basket in a most appealing way, but watch out for thorns if you site it near a doorway or walkway.

The miniature roses are dainty, twiggy plants that are ideal as the centrepiece of a basket and can take

problems. You may need to spray occasionally against troublesome blackspot and aphids. However, most modern varieties are robust despite their dainty appearance, and you should not experience any big problems.

Fuchsias and Pelargoniums

These woody-based plants are the mainstay of many a summer hanging basket, and rightly so. Few plants can rival their ease of cultivation and length of flowering season. They both usefully have a number of different forms. Upright cultivars are perfect as the central plant of a large basket, while trailing forms are excellent cascading down the sides.

PLANTS AT THEIR BEST IN SUMMER
Begonia
Bidens
Dorotheanthus
Fuchsia
Impatiens
Lobelia
Pelargonium
Petunias

Tender Perennials

This group of plants is growing in popularity and nurseries and garden centres offer new species and cultivars every year. In addition to the marvellous osteospermums, there are bidens, felicia and argyranthemum, all of which produce their vivid flowers over a long period.

Annuals

Hardy and half-hardy annuals are the mainstay of the summer garden, and most are easily grown from seed. Alternatively, they can be obtained as plugs or plantlets, ready to be planted out in early summer.

Above: Yellow-leaved lysimachia is an excellent trailing plant and a good substitute for ivy in a predominantly yellow basket.

Perhaps most familiar of all summer annuals are lobelias, trailing forms of which have been specially bred for containers. Colours include different shades of blue, as well as purple, with white and red. Equally noteworthy are the petunias, which can be found in a wide colour range, including white, yellow, cream, red and blue, with some bicolours. Double forms and those with ruffled petal edges are particularly appealing. Look out especially for the trailing types.

Foliage

At the height of summer a hanging basket can be virtually a ball of flowers, but don't underestimate the value of pure green to tone down a scheme. Ivies and periwinkles can be

Above: Pelargonium 'Eclipse' produces masses of pink flowers in large open heads.

24

relied on to give a long-lasting performance, to which can be added the tender helichrysums, with felted leaves of grey or soft lime green, or the pick-a-back plant (*Tolmiea menziesii*), with its fresh green, toothed leaves.

Summer Problems

While summer is the time for sitting back and enjoying the fruits of your labours in the garden at large, you cannot just relax and let your hanging baskets get on with it. They need care and attention. Tender leaves can easily scorch with too much sun, and flowers will rapidly fade. This is the ideal time – from the plant's point

GARDENER'S TIP

If the basket dries out, stand it on a bucket and give it a good soaking. Allow it to sit in the bucket until the compost (soil mix) is saturated. Adding a few drops of dishwashing detergent to the water will help water absorption.

of view – for setting seed. At this time you need to increase your watering, giving the basket a thorough soaking once or twice a day. If the weather is very hot, you might even need to move the basket to a more shady position. If you have baskets at the front and back of the house, swap them around every

Above: *Yellow-flowered bidens is a tender perennial that is often treated as an annual. It produces dainty flowers on trailing stems all summer long.*

25

few days, and turn them. Keep up the deadheading, or the flower display will be shortened. On the plus side, succulent plants, such as Livingstone daisies (*Dorotheanthus*), will positively revel in the heat and flower their hearts out, as will pelargoniums. Plants with aromatic leaves will release their oils now.

If you want your baskets to give pleasure throughout the season, look for plants that are in flower over a long period. Most floriferous of all are probably the pelargoniums, with flowers in shades of white, pink, salmon and red. The ivy-leaved

Above: *These osteospermums and diascias in subtle pastel colours are slightly tender but will carry on flowering until the first frosts appear.*

varieties are trailing, so are ideal for the sides of a basket, with perhaps a more upright cultivar at the centre. Fuchsias also have a long period of interest, often surviving into late autumn, and there are trailing as well as more upright cultivars.

Make sure you include some foliage plants, such as ivies and helichrysum, which will provide a solid background throughout the season.

All plants will flower for longer if regularly deadheaded. This diverts the plant's energy away from seed production and encourages it to produce further flowers.

Left: *Nasturtiums are among the easiest annuals to grow. 'Alaska' has the added attraction of variegated leaves.*

Things to Watch Out For

In a very hot spell baskets can easily dry out and delicate plants will scorch. Remember that their roots are well above ground level and hence can easily bake, because there is little moist soil to keep them cool. The problem is made worse if the basket is next to a wall that reflects the heat. A wall that has been in the sun for most of the afternoon will continue to radiate heat well into the evening when the sun is no longer on it. If necessary, take the basket to a position where it will be shaded when the sun is at its scorching strongest.

> **GARDENER'S TIP**
>
> Pelargoniums and many tender perennials can be over-wintered in a cool, light, frost-free place, such as an unheated bedroom or a porch (sunroom).

Flowering plants run to seed faster in hot weather, so keep up your deadheading regime. But remember that plants with succulent leaves, such as Livingstone daisies, will thrive in baking conditions. Most of the grey-leaved plants, especially those with fine hairs covering the leaves, will also flourish in hot weather.

Above: This riotous mix of fuchsias, lobelia, petunias, scarlet pelargoniums, nemesias and verbena has been planned for maximum impact.

AUTUMN BASKETS

A surprising number of plants are at their best in autumn. Shortening days bring cooler temperatures, and although there may not be as many flowers, they will last longer in the gentle autumn sun. Many annuals, particularly if sown late, will carry on until the first frosts, but others to enjoy later in the year include fruiting plants, such as bright red capsicums.

Annual capsicums, with their cheerful red, yellow or orange ball-like fruits, are appealing, as are the cultivars of *Gaulthesia mucronata*, the colourful fruits of which are beginning to ripen at this time of year to give additional interest to the basket.

Many members of the daisy family reach their peak at this time of year, and some dahlias and chrysanthemums make ideal basket plants. A dwarf chrysanthemum could be the central plant, surrounded by small ivies or possibly a late sowing of lobelias or helichrysum. This is also the season when the tuberous begonias are glorious, giving a show of colourful blooms. Look out especially for trailing cultivars such as 'Cascade Orange'.

Above: *Autumn is the season of the tuberous begonias, here partnered by pink diascias,* Helichrysum petiolare *and a fuchsia.*

Above: The perennial bidens can be relied on to produce its starry yellow flowers well into autumn.

diascias, will also continue to flower. A late feed will give all such plants a boost, but they will not survive the first autumn frosts. This is the time to look to the true plants of autumn, such as chrysanthemums, which produce satisfying mounds of colour, and sedums. Winter-flowering heathers will even provide colour into the darker days of winter.

GARDENER'S TIP

After flowering, dry off the tubers of begonias and store them over winter in a cool, dry, frost-free place for planting out again the following year. When new buds appear, you could propagate them by cutting the tubers in sections and planting them like cuttings.

Maintaining Interest

Autumn is an unpredictable season at the best of times. If the summer was cool and the autumn continues mild, many annuals will carry on flowering, provided they are deadheaded regularly. Many of the tender perennials, such as osteospermums, felicias and

---

PLANTS AT THEIR BEST IN AUTUMN

Calluna vulgaris
Capsicum annuum
Chrysanthemum
Fuchsia
Gaultheria mucronata
Impatiens
Sedum
Solenostemon

Above: With its perfectly formed flowers and arching habit, 'Dark Eyes' is an ideal fuchsia for a hanging basket.

WINTER BASKETS

It is possible to have colour and fragrance even in winter, but your choices are obviously more restricted then, since this is the time of year when most plants are resting. Winter-flowering pansies, invaluable though they are, will actually flower only during mild spells. For colour in the very depths of winter, you should look to the heathers (some of which have foliage that takes on attractive tints as the temperature dips) and dwarf berrying shrubs, such as gaultherias. The latter need lime-free (ericaceous) compost (soil mix), but winter heathers will tolerate lime.

PLANTS AT THEIR BEST
IN WINTER
Buxus
Erica carnea
Galanthus
Hedera
Skimmia japonica
Viola (winter-flowering)

This is also the time that the ivies come into their own. They exhibit a quite astonishing range of leaf shape (some being attractively crinkled at the edges) and variegation. Some are tinged pink or bronze in cold weather. A basket planted with ivies alone can be more attractive than you might think. You could even try tiny dwarf conifers or a hebe for leaf contrast. Small varieties of skimmia are also a possibility. Choose either a berrying female or the compact male form, 'Rubella', which has red-edged leaves and pink flower buds, which develop in autumn and last throughout winter, finally opening in spring. Plant them out in your garden the following year or pass them on to friends.

Left: Variegated ivies are an obvious choice for a winter basket, here livened up by yellow and bronze winter-flowering pansies.

Above: A hanging basket planted solely with one or two cultivars of small-leaved ivies will be a real eye-catcher once the plants are mature.

Danger Zones

Not only is the weather at its harshest in winter, but there is usually precious little light or sun. Although many plants tolerate wet and even a light covering of snow, evergreens in particular hate cold, drying winds, which will seriously damage their foliage if they do not kill the plant out-right. Make sure your baskets are not hanging in a wind funnel. At this time of year, it also makes sense to hang your baskets only in the most sheltered spots. If particularly severe weather is threatened, move your baskets under cover. Even the shelter of a porch or a covered car port should be sufficient to protect the plants and keep them in good health.

Above: A miniature clipped buxus *will provide sculptured interest and colour.*

Above: Erica *comes in a range of colours that will brighten up a winter basket.*

31

Hanging Baskets Indoors

If you are fortunate enough to have a conservatory, greenhouse or sunroom, you could grow plants that thrive in hanging baskets and can be kept in such situations all year round. In this way hanging baskets can be more than just a seasonal pleasure.

Plants for Indoor Baskets

The first choice for baskets indoors should be those plants that are actually airborne in the wild. These are the plants known as epiphytes, which cling to trees without actually deriving any nutrients from them. Many orchids come into this category, and there are plenty of modern hybrids that have been specially developed to tolerate the conditions found in the typical centrally heated home. Those

Above: With its trailing stems, this rainforest cactus makes an obvious choice for a hanging basket.

with trailing flower stems are especially well suited to baskets. Rainforest epiphytic cacti that can be grown in baskets include the familiar Christmas cactus (*Schlumbergera*) and cultivars of *Epiphyllum*. A few ferns are also natural tree-dwellers.

Trailing houseplants, such as wandering Jew (*Tradescantia*) and the popular spider plant (*Chlorophytum comosum*), are also worth including.

Above: The orchid Coelogyne flaccida *is well adapted to being above ground level and tolerates indoor conditions.*

PLANTS FOR INDOOR
HANGING BASKETS

Chlorophytum comosum
'Vittatum'
Nephrolepis exaltata
'Bostoniensis'
Orchids (epiphytic species)
Platycerium bifurcatum
Schlumbergera
Tradescantia fluminensis
'Albovittata'

Caring for Baskets Indoors

Rainforest plants are generally adapted to growing in low light levels and need to be shaded from hot sun. Conversely, most are best if they are given maximum light in winter, so be prepared to move your plants around or alter the shading of any window they are near. They will not tolerate freezing temperatures, so move them well away from the glass when the winter is at its coldest.

It is worth spending more to buy the special composts (soil mixes) that cacti and orchids require. These are usually very free-draining, since the plants are accustomed to free passage of air among the roots, and orchid compost usually contains bark.

Unless your baskets are suspended over a solid floor with a drain,

*Above: Graceful, arching ferns, such as the Boston fern (*Nephrolepis exaltata 'Bostoniensis'*), are ideal for baskets.*

watering can be a problem. The best solution is to mist them, twice a day or more when in active growth, and just occasionally in winter to keep the foliage plump and fresh looking. For the same reason, feed with a foliar feed rather than a root drench.

In summer you can move your hanging baskets to a cool, sheltered place outdoors. Gradual controlled exposure to outdoor conditions firms the growth and makes the plants more disease-resistant.

*Above: When it is slightly pot-bound, the spider plant (*Chlorophytum comosum*) will produce plantlets on trailing stems.*

> ### GARDENER'S TIP
> If you need to give your baskets a thorough watering, hang them in the shower, making sure the setting is at cold. Allow them to drain thoroughly before attempting to move them back to their permanent position.

Satisfying the Senses

PLANTS APPEAL TO OUR SENSES IN MORE THAN ONE WAY. WHILE WE ALL REJOICE IN THE COLOURS AND BEAUTY OF THEIR FLOWERS, WE SHOULD NEVER OVERLOOK THEIR MORE SUBTLE APPEAL TO OUR SENSES OF TOUCH, TASTE AND SMELL.

USING COLOUR

Colours make an immediate impact. Strong yellows, oranges and reds are known to increase the heartbeat slightly and are always considered exciting. Blues and pinks are more calming, and most restful and soothing to the eye of all is plain green.

Think of the position of the basket when you are choosing colours. Strong vibrant reds and yellows work best in

> ### GARDENER'S TIP
> When you choose a colour scheme remember that pale colours, such as pastel shades of blue, pink and yellow, tend to recede and appear further away, while strong oranges, reds and purples always seem to be nearer to the viewer and will dominate a display.

hot sun, but creams, pinks and lavenders tend to bleach out and look white. Conversely, pale colours will glow in half-light or shade, while deep reds and purples will look almost black.

Combining Colours

Use combinations of different colours as a painter would. Complementary colours (red and green; blue and orange; purple and yellow) tend to fizz when they are placed next to each other, making some exciting effects. If you add some grey to such a combination, in the form of foliage plants, it can soften the impact. If you decide to base a planting scheme on complementaries, however, it is best to avoid adding white, which tends to flare out, preventing the eye from finding a resting place.

Above: This riotous mix of sweet peas uses a range of colours together, harmonized by the abundance of fresh green leaves and stems.

34

Different tones of the same colour always look pleasing together. Creams and apricots blend happily with oranges and reds, for instance, as do lavenders and mauves with purples. Clear red and blue seldom make good bedfellows, but a rich purple can be enlivened with the right shade of red. You will soon learn what works.

If you are using a combination of pinks, try not to mix those that tend towards blue with those that have some orange in them. Try the bluish pinks with warm mauve and purples, and the orange-pinks with red and yellow. Potential clashes can always be softened by the use of plain green or grey foliage.

Above: *The vivid colours of nasturtiums and French marigolds combine to create an eyecatching arrangement.*

Below: *The begonias and diascias used here could have clashed were it not for the presence of the ever-dependable* Helichrysum petiolare.

Dramatic Effects

Bearing in mind the effects the different colours have on the senses, the most dramatic plantings involve rich, deep, saturated colours, such as purple, orange, yellow and red. A typical planting might involve a richly coloured petunia or fuchsia – several cultivars have red or purple flowers – surrounded by dark blue, trailing lobelias with a few orange and red nasturtiums tucked in for added vibrancy. Purple on its own, or as the principal colour, would certainly be dramatic, but if you are mixing purples

> STRIKINGLY COLOURED PLANTS
>
> *Antirrhinum*
> *Fuchsia*
> *Lobelia*
> *Nasturtium*
> *Pelargonium*
> *Petunia*
> *Verbena*
> *Viola*

beware: red-purples and blue-purples make unhappy bedfellows. Play for safety and include plants with grey foliage or some ivies, which will bring a welcome calming note to the scheme.

Above: Pink flowers are always enhanced by silver-grey foliage, and these warm pink pelargoniums and diascias make a beautifully subtle planting with Helichrysum petiolare.

Above: The combination of a virginal white pelargonium with purple daisies and verbenas is undeniably romantic.

Above: As well as the familiar strident colours, busy Lizzies come in some lovely soft shades.

Soothing Schemes

For subtlety, choose pastels. Creams, pinks, blues and lavenders always work well together, though the results can be insipid unless you include a few deeper shades of those colours. In theory, white should be the most calming of all, and silver and white baskets are undeniably romantic, but again you have to be careful where you place them. In full sun, the flowers tend to bleach, and a subtle scheme might end up looking washed out. On the whole, white flowers are best used to highlight other pale colours.

A simple planting might surround a pale fuchsia (there is no clear white, but some of the pink varieties are very pale) or pelargonium with white lobelias and cream, lavender or white petunias. The ever-reliable grey-leaved *Helichrysum petiolare* could give the planting substance. You can warm up a cool scheme by using pinks with a touch of orange in them – a colour usually called salmon. Diascias are among the most desirable, many having flowers of a smoky apricot.

PLANTS WITH PALE
FLOWERS

Diascia
Fuchsia
Lobelia
Nemesia
Osteospermum
Pelargonium
Petunia
Viola

Using Foliage

Although most planting schemes are usually planned around the flowers, you could plant a basket for the appeal of foliage, either on its own, for a subtle look, or combined with a mixture of flowering plants. A dramatic combination would be black lilyturf (*Ophiopogon nigrescens*) mixed with silver-leaved *Helichrysum petiolare*. Blue fescue (*Festuca glauca*) would be a more understated alternative. For richer, bolder effects, annual coleus (*Solenostemon*) would give as vivid a display as any combination of flowers and over a much longer period. Coleus seedlings vary and can never be accurately predicted in advance, but colours include red, brown and gold. Foliage begonias (*Begonia rex*) have

> ### PLANTS WITH SILVER OR GREY FOLIAGE
> *Artemisia*
> *Dianthus*
> *Festuca glauca*
> *Helianthemum* 'The Bride'
> *Helichrysum petiolare*
> *Nepeta*
> *Santolina*
> *Senecio*
> *Stachys byzantina*

beautiful purple or silver leaves with a pronounced metallic sheen.

Be careful where you place baskets planted for foliage effect, however. Most need some sun to enhance the colour, but the leaves can scorch in too hot a position – somewhere sheltered from the midday sun is usually best.

The ever-popular spider plant (*Chlorophytum comosum* 'Vittatum') is generally grown as a houseplant, but there is no reason not to allow it an excursion outdoors in the frost-free months. It is an ideal basket plant, with striped, arching stems that carry new plantlets at their tips, each of which is a potential new plant.

Left: A sumptuous combination of purple heuchera, orange and brown pansies, mimulus and golden lysimachia. The purple foliage sets off the pansies.

Above: The green foliage of Helichrysum petiolare *'Aureum' makes a striking partner to blue anagallis and pansies.*

Combining Foliage with Flowers

For the best of both worlds, try blending foliage plants with flowering ones. Alaska Series nasturtiums solve the problem in one, because the leaves, which are beautifully marbled with splashes of pink and cream, are almost as appealing as the orange, yellow and red flowers. Otherwise, try matching leaf colour with flower colour. An ivy with cream variegated foliage will echo any cream flowers you may have chosen, for instance. The yellow-leaved *Lysimachia nummularia* 'Aurea' works splendidly as a foil to red and orange flowers and is a dramatic complement to purple verbenas, but take care when combining it with other shades of yellow – you should experiment with different shades to find out what works best. Purple- and bronze-leaved plants are also striking when used in conjunction with red or yellow flowers. For a more sophisticated effect, try combining them with cream or white flowers.

If you like variegated plants it is probably best to stick to one variety only in each basket, combined with plain-leaved plants as a foil. If you include too much variegation there is a danger of creating a visually confusing look, whereas with a single, well-chosen variety you can ensure maximum effect.

PLANTS WITH COLOURED FOLIAGE

Begonia rex
Chlorophytum comosum 'Vittatum'
Festuca glauca
Fuchsia 'Autumnale'
Gynura
Hedera (variegated forms)
Helichrysum
Lysimachia nummularia 'Aurea'
Ophiopogon nigrescens
Solenostemon (annual)
Tradescantia fluminensis 'Albovittata'
Tropaeolum Alaska Series

INTRODUCING SCENT

The scent of plants is as important a part of their appeal as is the colour of their flowers, and you may wish to plant a few baskets with this as the principal theme. A minority of plants have a distinctly unpleasant smell, but many have a potent fragrance that promotes a sense of well-being.

Some flowers have a scent that is emitted only at certain times of the day – when their natural pollinators are active. Night-scented plants, such as *Nicotiana*, for instance, are usually pollinated by nocturnal moths. Scents can also vary in intensity at different times of day according to the moisture content of the atmosphere. Roses are often at their sweetest when the dew hangs in the air.

Above: Baskets filled with fragrant ground-cover roses make a summer focal point at the end of the pergola.

Types of Scent

Scent is the most elusive of the senses and not everybody reacts in the same way to particular fragrances. For some, they awake precious memories stored up from childhood, while others are completely indifferent to them. One gardener might find that a particular scent has strong and positive associations while another might be completely unmoved by it.

Citrus smells are light and refreshing, while herbal scents such as thyme and lavender tend to be calming and relaxing. Some herbal scents are more astringent and often have notes of eucalyptus that not everyone finds pleasing, although many people experience them as invigorating. Musky scents can be very provocative, though these essences are rare in the plant world. Some flower scents combine more than one note and often seem to be 'layered'. Such scents, which we usually think of as exotic, are so rich and heady as to be almost cloying, though undeniably intoxicating. The commonest scents in the garden are usually defined as aromatic. They are usually sweetly spicy and always appealing, and we seem never to tire of them. They are often found in the distinctly almond-like fragrance of heliotropes and the warm clove scent of old-fashioned carnations and pinks. Violet scents are sharper and more fatiguing but also more transitory. Mignonettes (*Reseda*) and *Iris reticulata* as well as violets have scents in this group.

Rose scents are usually fruity and spicy, pleasing both up close and at a distance. They are best in a sunny spot where the warmth brings out their fragrance. Some varieties of tulips as well as roses have these lovely scents. Interestingly, many of the roses have scents that seem to belong to a further group, the citrus or lemon group. These scents are almost universally perceived as pleasant and exhilarating rather than calming. Distinctive honey-scented tones are occasionally

Above: Few pansies are scented, but orange forms are sometimes fragrant, recalling their link to sweet violets.

detected in plants and their fragrance is warm and enduring. They are most commonly found among the orchids.

Above: White Lobularia maritima *has a delicate, pleasing scent that gives this simple scheme an added appeal.*

Positioning Scented Plants

Bearing in mind the power of scent, you need to think carefully where you place hanging baskets containing scented plants. While it is a joy to fling open a window and breathe in a heady mix of roses and jasmine, you may find such smells too cloying if they are near a bedroom window that is open on hot, sultry nights. Nevertheless, a basket of predominantly night-scented plants can be a pleasing addition to a pergola over a paved area where you dine *al fresco* on balmy summer evenings.

Plants with aromatic leaves, such as most of the herbs, especially woody-stemmed ones like artemisia, lavender and rosemary, are richest in their essential oils at the height of summer, and these tend to be released only when they are crushed. Site these in full sun somewhere where you regularly pass by, perhaps near a doorway or suspended from a garden arch, so that you can reach up and rub a few leaves between your finger and thumb to release their fragrance. Hanging them near a barbecue area will allow you to

Above: Include some late-flowering narcissi with Anemone blanda *and ivy for a fragrant spring display. Make sure you hang the basket where you can appreciate the scent.*

Above: Dwarf lavender has scented grey leaves as well as strongly fragrant flowers. It prefers a sunny site.

Above: Blue petunias, here planted against a sunny wall, often have a rich scent not found in the other colours.

have material close at hand to garnish grilled steaks, lamb or fish or simply to fling on the flames to release their evocative aroma.

Heavy scents, of the kind found in such plants as jasmine and stephanotis, are rich and penetrating and are delicious when caught on the passing breeze. Within the confines of a green-house or conservatory, or in the house itself, they can be overpowering. For fragrance indoors, you could consider growing some of the *Dendrobium* or *Coelogyne* orchid hybrids or *Cyclamen persicum* hybrids, but note that not all of these are scented. Look for plants in flower and sniff out their potential before you make a purchase.

SCENTED PLANTS

Convallaria majalis
Crocus (some)
Cyclamen persicum
Dianthus
Iris (some)
Lathyrus odoratus
Lavandula
Lobularia maritima
Muscari armeniacum
Narcissus (some)
Nicotiana
Petunia (some)
Pelargonium (scented-leaved)
Phlox
Reseda odorata
Rosmarinus
Narcissus (some)
Primula (some)
Tulipa (some)
Verbena

Benefits of Scented Plants

Scented plants have the inestimable value of attracting beneficial insects, such as hoverflies and ladybirds (ladybugs), into the garden. A healthy ladybird population will help keep aphids at bay, since they feed on these pests. The poached egg plant (*Limnanthes douglasii*), with its saucer-shaped, yellow and white flowers, will be alive with bees throughout summer. Butterflies are an ornament to the garden in their own right.

Many plants are believed to have healing qualities, and they have been used in traditional medicines for centuries. A cup of mint tea helps settle the stomach after a meal, while an infusion of lemon balm can be very soothing. Feverfew is said to alleviate

Above: Lavandula stoechas *ssp.* pedunculata *is a form of lavender from Provence that is particularly attractive to bees.*

headaches and migraines, but no herb other than the familiar culinary ones should be taken in any form for its health benefits without consulting a medical practitioner.

Citronella oil is widely used as a component of insect repellents. Growing citrus-scented plants, such as lemon balm (*Melissa officinalis*), in a basket near a favourite evening sitting place may help to deter mosquitoes and other unwelcome night-time insects provided you rub its leaves periodically to release the lemon scent.

Left: The silver-leaved thyme is a strong feature of this basket and will be alive with bees when it is in flower.

Combining Scented Plants

Placing two or three scented plants together can be detrimental to the effect of each and can confuse the nose. You will achieve the most pleasing results by restricting yourself to one scented plant in each basket, particularly if the scent is a heavy one. However, the aromatic herbs and scented-leaved plants, such as pelargoniums, which are fragrant only when bruised, can work well together, because you have some control over when the scent is actually released. In a mixed basket, a succession of scents is possible. The leaves of some nasturtiums (*Tropaeolum*), for instance, have a fresh, peppery scent when young, and this could be enjoyed before later, scented flowers – pansies or petunias,

Above: An elegant planting with an added dimension: the scent of the purple lobularias will attract a host of insects.

for example – appear. Alternatively, use these plants with herbs or pelargoniums that owe their scent to aromatic oils, which are at their richest when the weather is hottest – from mid- to late summer. Misting the plants will help to release their fragrance.

PLANTS THAT ATTRACT BEES AND BUTTERFLIES

Aster (dwarf forms)
Aubrieta deltoides
Lavandula species
Limnanthes douglasii
Lobularia maritima
Sedum 'Vera Jameson'
Thymus species
Viola tricolor

Left: In addition to the beauty of its abundant mauve flowers, Pelargonium *'Little Gem' has the advantage of soft-textured, lobed leaves, which exude a warm, rose-lemon fragrance.*

PLANTS TO TOUCH

Good gardeners love to handle their plants, some of which seem to grow just to be touched, especially those with furry or silky leaves and those with aromatic leaves that release their fragrance when bruised. This characteristic is, perhaps, the subtlest of pleasures that plants can give us, and appreciation of it is one to be encouraged. Some people believe that plants that are caressed regularly grow more vigorously and are more disease-resistant, although it is obviously difficult to demonstrate this scientifically. Touching may imitate the contact that plants would receive in the wild from passing animal life.

> ### PLANTS WITH TEXTURAL LEAVES
>
> *Fuchsia* (triphylla types)
> *Gynura*
> *Helichrysum*
> *Pelargonium* (scented-leaved)
> *Rosmarinus*
> *Stachys byzantina*

Leaf Texture

Waxy and furry coatings to leaves developed as a response to climate, to protect the plants from hot sun by helping the leaf to retain moisture. Such textures are at their most pronounced, therefore, when the sun is at its hottest, so a basket featuring these is best sited in a sunny position that will encourage the plants to build up their protective coatings.

Plants with smooth, waxy leaves include, most obviously, succulent plants such as *Schlumbergera*. The nearest hardy equivalents are the sedums, with their fleshy, almost glassy leaves, which can assume a grape-like bloom as the temperature rises. Furry-textured leaves have an irresistible appeal to children, who love to stroke the charmingly and aptly named lambs' ears (*Stachys byzantina*), which is usually used to edge a

Above: *The leaves of the triphylla-type fuchsia 'Thalia' – at the centre of the basket and yet to bear its orange flowers – are velvety and eminently strokeable.*

flower border but also makes an excellent basket plant, particularly in one of its non-flowering forms such as 'Silver Carpet'. *Helichrysum petiolare* also has soft, velvety leaves, though they are firmer-textured and, being smaller, not quite so easy to stroke. An attractive alternative is *Convolvulus cneorum*, with its silky-textured, silver-grey leaves that are no less appealing than the glistening white, funnel-shaped flowers. This is actually a Mediterranean shrub, but its lax habit makes it perfect for a basket.

Leaves that are soft, thin and silky usually need some shelter from hot sun, and most will do best in shade. Triphylla-type fuchsias are outstanding here, with large, usually bronze-flushed leaves with a metallic sheen. *Gynura aurantiaca* 'Purple Passion' has purple hairy leaves that shine almost blue, making a strong appeal to our tactile sense. Popular as a houseplant, there is no reason this should not find its way into a hanging basket outdoors provided there are no great temperature fluctuations and it is sheltered from any strong winds. Another useful trailing foliage plant is wandering Jew (*Tradescantia*). Their leaves have a glittering crystallized appearance, almost as though they have been lightly sprinkled with sugar.

Above: *The yellow leaves of* Helichrysum petiolare *'Limelight' bring their distinctive texture to a colourful summer basket.*

EDIBLE PLEASURES

In an age when commercial crops are routinely sprayed against pests and diseases and fed with chemicals to increase crop size and extend shelf life, many gardeners are attracted to the idea of growing their own fruit and vegetables at home. You do not have to have a large area of flat ground, as you might imagine, and growing edible crops in hanging baskets is actually a very practical option if you have only limited space. This way you can be sure that they are always ready to hand to be picked. Moreover, home-grown crops are always tastier and fresher than their shop-bought equivalents.

Make sure that your edible baskets are positioned near to the kitchen so that you do not have too far to walk in wet weather. Remember, though, that all vegetables need an open, sunny site to grow properly, so if the area near your kitchen door is shady, you may need to hang your basket elsewhere for the best crops.

What to Grow

Look out for quick-maturing, dwarf, trailing forms that have been specially developed to meet the needs of gardeners with limited space. All edible crops are greedy plants so will need a lot of feeding to give you the results you want. Lettuces and other salad leaves are an ideal crop for growing in hanging baskets. 'Little Gem' is a reliable dwarf variety. The cut-and-come-again varieties, such as 'Frisby', are particularly useful, because you can simply snip off the leaves you need for a salad and the plant will carry on producing more, so you do not have to remove a whole plant at a time. Some are decorative in their own right, with red or crinkly-edged leaves.

Above: The pretty flowers of the trailing tomato plants, here combined with nasturtiums (also edible), give a hint of tasty crops to come.

Cherry tomatoes are also an excellent choice and, of course, look very

Left: This sumptuous basket combines perennial herbs with fragrant flowers.

that is truly beautiful to look at, as well as a valued food source. Beware of overplanting the basket, however. If the vegetables have to compete for the water and nutrients, they may not produce the tasty crops you want.

Maintaining the Basket

The demands of the majority of vegetables are much greater than those of flowering plants, which should be considered when deciding what to grow. They need a free-draining compost (soil mix), so choose a lightweight type that will not compact with the frequent watering. Because free-draining composts tend to be low in nutrients, and vegetables demand greater amounts of fertilizer, feed the baskets with a soluble variety. Tomato fertilizers are quite high in potassium, to promote good fruiting, but tend to encourage other leafy vegetables, such as lettuces, to bolt. For these, look for a high-nitrogen feed. If the idea of using chemicals to enhance an edible crop does not appeal, there are also organic equivalents, usually based on seaweed extract. Apply all fertilizers at the manufacturer's recommended rate. Overfeeding (and overwatering) can impair the flavour of the crop.

attractive as the cherry-like fruits ripen in late summer. 'Tumbler' is the cultivar generally recommended.

Beans have the advantage of pretty flowers before the beans form. Be sure to harvest the beans regularly while they are still small and sweet. Older beans will be tough and stringy. Sadly, root crops, such as carrots, parsnips and potatoes, are definitely not suitable for such a limited space. They need a deeper root run than it is possible to achieve in a hanging basket.

You could try adding some flowers to the planting, to create a basket

---

GARDENER'S TIP

Seed merchants bring out new varieties every year, so check their catalogues for the latest additions. For success with edible crops, use baskets no less than 35cm (14in) in diameter.

Growing Herbs

If you do not have a herb garden – or even if you do – you might like to grow some herbs in a basket that you can hang near the back door or kitchen window so that they are always within reach. Held aloft as they are, hanging baskets offer what most herbs need above all – good drainage. Unlike many other plants, herbs thrive in relatively poor soil, so feed less often than you would a flowering basket. However, you will need a very free-draining compost (soil mix), so be sure to add perlite or vermiculite so that there is no danger of waterlogging.

Some herbs are perennials, which means that the basket can be a year-round feature. You can also include herbs in mixed baskets – sage and parsley make particularly attractive additions to flower baskets. It would be a practical idea to grow basil with tomatoes, because the two flavours complement each other so nicely, and you would have the ingredients of a tasty salad growing together.

Nearly all the herbs that are suitable for hanging baskets are sun-lovers. Indeed, sun is often needed to enhance their aromatic properties. Most have tough leaves – sage, lavender

Below: With its crops of parsley, sage and tarragon, this basket is every cook's dream. It will produce fresh leaves over a long period of time if trimmed regularly.

Above: Chives have pretty flowers, but if you want to reserve your plants solely for culinary use, it is best to nip them off before they are fully formed.

and rosemary – but those with more delicate leaves, such as basil and tarragon, may need some shelter from the midday sun during the hotter months. The exception is mint, which is not only shade-tolerant but demands reliably moist soil if it is to prosper. Make sure that you keep mint baskets well watered.

Maintaining a Supply

Herbs actually benefit from being harvested regularly. Not only does this keep the plants neat and compact, but it prevents them from flowering and setting seed and makes them put out fresh young leaves, always the most tender and tasty. Basil and parsley are annual herbs, which tend to become coarse if allowed to bolt and lose their characteristic flavour. If you pick from them regularly to provide garnishes,

they are unlikely to run to seed, but if flowers should begin to form, nip them out with finger and thumb or scissors.

You might, however, allow herbs such as lavender, rosemary and thyme to flower. Not only are the flowers pretty in themselves, but they will provide a valuable nectar source for bees and other pollinating insects.

HERBS FOR A HANGING BASKET

Basil (annual)
Chives
Lavender
Parsley (annual)
Rosemary (prostrate varieties)
Sage

Above: Herbs can please the eye as much as the taste buds. This striking scheme combines mint, parsley, lavender and thymes with alpine pinks.

51

Growing Strawberries

Believe it or not, you can even grow strawberries in hanging baskets, and at least you can be sure you'll experience no problems with mice, the scourge of many a fruit garden. Pick and choose among the varieties. Alpine strawberries are the best, being naturally small and neat-growing, but you could also experiment with some of the larger fruited varieties. All strawberries have the additional attraction of white flowers in spring.

You can either raise plants from seed or buy plantlets, probably the better option if you are short of time. Look for compact cultivars. You will have most success with those that are recommended for container growing.

It is also worth checking when the cropping season is. Some fruit in early summer, others in midsummer, while a third group provides late crops. A few varieties produce relatively small crops but over a long period, and these may be the best choice for a busy town-dweller. Make sure that any variety you choose is self-fertile, unless there are other strawberry plants grown nearby.

Below: Two types of strawberry are used here, the large-fruited 'Maxim' and smaller alpine plants. A crimson pelargonium adds a dash more colour.

Above: This half basket uses attractive alpine strawberries almost as much for the appeal of their foliage as for their fruits. Red petunias and a variegated helichrysum sit above them.

Strawberries are susceptible to mildew, a common fungal infection encouraged by high humidity and fluctuating temperatures – the kind of conditions that often prevail in late summer and autumn. Spray at the first sign of disease, but make sure that any product you use will not taint the fruit or damage wildlife.

Even if you can't grow a large enough crop to make preserves, you can still have alpine strawberries to add to your breakfast cereal or cornflakes in the summer or to make tiny pots of compote for enjoying with scones (biscuits) and cream. Alpine strawberries are also traditionally eaten in France dropped in a glass of champagne – a custom certainly well worth importing.

RECOMMENDED STRAWBERRIES

'Calypso' (perpetual-fruiting)
'Mignonette' (alpine)
'Temptation' (perpetual-fruiting)

Planting Combinations

You need not restrict yourself to one strawberry cultivar, but two or three is probably the maximum you will manage in one basket. Allow an alpine strawberry to trail at the edges of the basket and place a larger fruited type in the centre of the compost (soil mix).

Strawberries are such attractive fruits that they can be used in conjunction with flowers for a display that is as much for the eye as the taste buds. Small pelargoniums, petunias or nasturtiums are possibilities, and if you stick to shades of red you can be sure to have a vivid display. There are also a few white strawberry cultivars, which would look charming mixed with a few cream petunias.

GARDENER'S TIP

Most strawberries ripen best in an open, sunny site. Alpine strawberries, however, will ripen perfectly well in light shade, so if the only position available is shaded, restrict yourself to these varieties. As the fruits begin to ripen, protect strawberry baskets with a piece of netting, otherwise the birds may help themselves to the entire crop.

Edible Flowers

Some flowers are edible and make colourful additions to salads and drinks. A bowl of chilled punch at a summer party will be considerably enhanced by the presence of a few viola or borage flowers floating on the surface, and they can also be used to garnish desserts, either fresh from the plant or given a coating of egg white and sugar. Flowers for culinary use are best picked when they have just opened, but before they are fully open and beginning to fade. If you have used chemicals against pests and diseases, make sure that all leaves and flowers are thoroughly washed before using them in the kitchen.

> **GARDENER'S TIP**
>
> Pick flowers on a sunny day before noon for the strongest concentration of essential oils.

Borage flowers can also be frozen in ice cubes to add to drinks, allowing you to revisit in a modest way the pleasures of summer once the plants that produced the flowers are spent. Place individual flowers in each compartment of an ice tray and fill with water. Once frozen, release the

Below: Leaving aside the blue felicia, this chirpy planting provides parsley leaves as well as marigold flowers, both of which can be used in the kitchen.

cubes from the trays and bag them up separately for storing in the freezer.

Nasturtium flowers can be used as a last-minute garnish to salads and have a fresh, peppery taste. Pansy flowers have a less distinctive flavour, but they have a lovely velvety texture.

Rose or marigold petals can be used to flavour butters or to scent oils and vinegars, adding to the appeal of your salad dressings. Soften butter (preferably unsalted) first and gently mash the flowers into it. The idea is to release some of the oils into the butter while preserving the integrity of the flowers. Flavoured butters are best used fresh, before the flowers discolour, otherwise the butter turns rancid.

Oils and vinegars act as preservatives, so have a longer shelf life than butter. Choose a lightly flavoured oil, such as sunflower. Wine or cider vinegar should be gently warmed before adding the flowers. Steep for two weeks on a sunny windowsill, shaking occasionally, then strain the liquid.

The petals of pot marigolds (*Calendula*) can be used to colour rice in place of saffron but will not impart any flavour. To dry marigold petals, lay the individual flowers on sheets of

Above: Not only can nasturtium leaves and flowers be used in salads and cooked dishes, but the seeds can also be pickled.

absorbent kitchen paper and allow them to dry naturally in a well-ventilated area. Once dry, pull the petals from the centre of the flower (which can then be discarded) and store them in an airtight screwtop jar.

To keep your plants producing new flowers, remove faded ones promptly.

Combining Plants

Using edible flowers in conjunction with other edible plants means that your useful baskets can be as attractive to look at as baskets planted for appearance alone. Try marigolds with nasturtiums, for instance, with a few added parsley plants for bulk. This type of planting also gives you more scope for variations in colour, flower and leaf shape and scent.

EDIBLE FLOWERS

Borago officinalis
Calendula
Rosa
Tropaeolum
Viola

55

Seasonal Tasks

GOOD TIME-MANAGEMENT WILL HELP YOU SUCCEED WITH HANGING BASKETS. THE FOLLOWING CALENDAR PROVIDES A TIMETABLE THAT WILL ENABLE YOU TO KEEP PACE WITH TASKS AS THEY NEED TO BE DONE, AND TO MAINTAIN HEALTHY BASKETS ALL YEAR ROUND.

SPRING

Early spring
- plant up evergreens, such as herbs and ivies, for a permanent display
- tidy up permanent plantings and remove any dead leaves
- sow seed of vegetables under protection
- coax overwintered fuchsias, pelargoniums and chrysanthemums back into growth with bottom heat if necessary
- take cuttings of overwintered fuchsias and chrysanthemums as they come into growth

Mid-spring
- plant herbs and ivies for a permanent display
- sow seed of flowering annuals, such as nasturtiums and marigolds
- sow seed of annual herbs, such as basil and parsley
- bring dormant begonia tubers back into life
- prune woody plants such as roses
- lightly trim evergreen herbs

Late spring
- start feeding permanent plantings as they come back into growth
- buy bedding plants suitable for baskets from garden centres
- plant up baskets for summer interest
- pot up spent bulbs for use the following year or plant out in the garden

Above: *A cheery display for a spring basket.*

Above: *A glorious summer combination.*

SUMMER

Early summer
• make late sowings of annuals for autumn baskets
• start feeding summer baskets with a high-potash fertilizer
• order bulbs from bulb suppliers for planting in autumn

Midsummer
• begin harvesting cut-and-come-again crops
• begin harvesting dwarf beans
• begin harvesting strawberries
• begin harvesting annual herbs
• sow seed of winter pansies and keep the seedlings cool
• deadhead flowering plants to keep up the display

Late summer
• take cuttings of herbs and other woody plants for overwintering
• take cuttings of tender perennials for overwintering
• continue harvesting strawberries

AUTUMN

• sow seed of hardy annuals for early flowers the following season
• sow seed of biennials, such as *Myosotis,* for an early spring display in 18 months
• gradually dry off fuchsias and pelargoniums for overwintering
• dry off begonia tubers and store dry over winter
• plant up baskets of dwarf bulbs

WINTER

• order seed of annuals and vegetables from seed catalogues
• order strawberry plants from commercial suppliers
• protect permanent plantings from heavy frosts
• continue to care for baskets indoors, watering to keep them just moist

Above: *Fuchsias provide colour in autumn.*   **Above:** *An evergreen basket for winter.*

Best Hanging Basket Plants

THIS QUICK REFERENCE CHART CAN BE USED TO SELECT THE MOST SUITABLE PLANTS FOR YOUR HANGING BASKETS IN TERMS OF THEIR REQUIREMENTS AND SEASON OF INTEREST. NOTE PARTICULARLY THE PLANTS' PREFERENCES FOR SUN OR SHADE.

Plant name	Height	Flower colour	Season of interest
Allium schoenoprasum FS	25cm (10in)	herb	spring/summer
Anagallis Tr FS	10cm (4in)	blue, red, pink	spring/summer
Antirrhinum hh FS	30cm (12in)	pink, red, purple, yellow, bronze, orange, white	summer
Argyranthemum fh FS	30cm (12in)	white, pink	summer/autumn
Asarina Tr FS	5cm (2in)	purple	summer
Aster FS	25cm (10in)	white, pink, violet, purple, red	summer/autumn
Begonia t Tr S/PS (tuberous and semperflorens)	20–60cm (8–24in)	white, yellow, orange, red	summer/autumn
Bellis perennis FS	15cm (6in)	white, pink, red	spring
Bidens fh Tr FS	25cm (10in)	yellow	summer
Buxus FS/S	15cm (6in)	foliage	all year
Calendula officinalis FS	25cm (10in)	cream, yellow, orange	summer
Calluna FS	15cm (6in)	white, pink, purple, crimson	summer/autumn
Chamaemelum FS	10cm (4in)	foliage	all year

Plant name	Height	Flower colour	Season of interest
Chlorophytum comosum t Tr S/PS	25cm (10in)	foliage	all year
Convallaria majalis Sh	20cm (8in)	white	spring
Crocus FS	10cm (4in)	white, yellow, purple, lilac	late winter/spring
Diascia FS Tr	30cm (12in)	pink, lilac, apricot	summer
Dwarf beans FS	30cm (12in)	vegetable	summer
Erica FS	30cm (12in)	white, pink, purple	winter/spring
Eschscholzia FS	30cm (12in)	cream, pink, orange, white, red, yellow	summer
Felicia t FS Tr	25cm (10in)	blue	summer
Fuchsia hh S/PS Tr (some)	25cm (10in)	pink, red, purple	summer/autumn
Galanthus officinalis S/PS	15cm (6in)	white	late winter
Glechoma hederacea 'Variegata' FS/S/PS Tr	15cm (6in)	foliage	all year
Gynura aurantiaca t S/PS Tr	30cm (12in)	foliage	all year
Gypsophila FS Tr	30cm (12in)	white	summer
Hedera (small-leaved) FS/Sh Tr	15cm (6in)	foliage	all year
Helichrysum petiolare hh FS Tr	15cm (6in)	foliage	all year
Impatiens t S/PS/Sh Tr (some)	15cm (6in)	white, pink, red	summer/autumn
Lathyrus odoratus FS Tr	25cm (10in)	white, pink, red, violet	summer
Lavandula FS	45cm (18in)	blue, purple	all year

Plant name	Height	Flower colour	Season of interest
Lobelia hh S/PS/Sh Tr (some)	10cm (4in)	white, blue, purple, red	summer
Lobularia maritima FS	10cm (4in)	white, purple	summer
Lysimachia nummularia 'Aurea' S/PS Tr	5cm (2in)	foliage	all year
Mentha Sh	45cm (18in)	herb	spring/summer/autumn
Mimulus S/PS Tr (some)	15cm (6in)	yellow, orange, red, pink	summer
Muscari armeniacum FS	12cm (5in)	purple, white	spring
Myosotis FS	30cm (12in)	blue	spring
Narcissus FS	15–30cm (6–12in)	white, cream, yellow	spring
Nemesia hh FS	20cm (8in)	cream, orange, pink, blue, purple, yellow	summer
Ocimum basilicum hh FS	25cm (10in)	herb	summer
Orchids t Sh Tr (some)	30cm (12in)	all colours	any time of year
Pelargonium t FS/S/PS Tr (some)	30cm (12in)	white, pink, red	summer
Petunia hh FS Tr	20cm (8in)	white, purple, blue, red	summer
Primula S/PS	15cm (6in)	white, pink, yellow, red, orange, purple	spring
Rosa (miniature and ground-cover) FS	25cm (10in)	white, pink, yellow, red, orange	summer/autumn
Rosmarinus officinalis FS Tr (some)	30cm (12in)	herb	all year

Plant name	Height	Flower colour	Season of interest
Salpiglossis hh FS	45cm (18in)	yellow, orange, red, purple, blue	summer
Salvia officinalis FS	30cm (12in)	herb	all year
Schlumbergera t S/PS Tr	20cm (8in)	red, pink, white	winter
Solenostemon hh S/PS	30cm (12in)	foliage	spring/summer/autumn
Strawberries FS Tr	12cm (5in)	fruit	summer
Tanacetum parthenium FS	45cm (18in)	white	summer
Thymus vulgaris FS	12cm (5in)	herb	all year
Tomatoes hh FS Tr (some)	15cm (6in)	fruiting vegetable	summer
Tradescantia t S/PS	20cm (8in)	foliage	all year
Tropaeolum FS Tr (some)	20cm (8in)	yellow, orange, red	summer
Verbena hh FS Tr	25cm (10in)	red, pink, blue, mauve, white	summer
Vinca S/PS/Sh Tr	15cm (6in)	white, blue, purple	foliage all year
Viola FS/S/PS	20cm (8in)	white, violet, yellow, orange, maroon, black	spring/summer/autumn/winter

KEY TO SYMBOLS

t = tender (needs minimum 5°C/41°F)

hh = half hardy
(survives lows of 0°C/32°F)

fh = frost hardy
(survives lows of -5°C/23°F)

Unmarked plants are fully hardy
(down to -15°C/5°F)

FS = full sun

S/PS = sun/partial shade
(i.e. best protected from hot sun)

Sh = shade

Tr = trailing

Common Names of Plants

alyssum *Lobularia maritima*

annual pepper *Capsicum annuum*

baby's breath *Gypsophila*

basil *Ocimum basilicum*

blue daisy *Felicia*

borage *borago officinalis*

box *Buxus*

busy Lizzie *Impatiens*

california poppy *Eschscholzia*

chamomile *Chamaemelum*

chives *Allium schoenoprasum*

christmas cactus *Schlumbergera*

coleus *Solenostemon*

creeping Jenny *Lysimachia nummularia*

daffodil *Narcissus*

daisy *Bellis perennis*

feverfew *Tanacetum parthenium*

forget-me-not *Myosotis*

French marigolds *Tagetes patula*

geranium *Pelargonium*

grape hyacinth *Muscari armeniacum*

ground ivy *Glechoma hederacea*

heather *Erica, Calluna*

ivy *Hedera helix*

lavender *Lavandula*

lemon balm *Melissa officinalis*

lily-of-the-valley *Convallaria majalis*

marguerite *Argyranthemum*

michaelmas daisy *Aster novae-angliae* and *A. novi-belgii*

mint *Mentha*

monkey flower *Mimulus*

nasturtium *Tropaeolum majus*

pansy *Viola* x *wittrockiana*

periwinkle *Vinca*

pimpernel *Anagallis*

pink *Dianthus*

polyanthus *Primula*

pot marigold *Calendula officinalis*

primrose *Primula vulgaris*

purple velvet plant *Gynura aurantiaca*

rose *Rosa*

rosemary *Rosmarinus officinalis*

sage *Salvia officinalis*

snapdragon *Antirrhinum*

snowdrop *Galanthus officinalis*

spider plant *Chlorophytum comosum*

sweet pea *Lathyrus odoratus*

sweet violet *Viola odorata*

thyme *Thymus vulgaris*

tobacco plant *Nicotiana*

tulip *tulipa*

wandering Jew *Tradescantia*

Above: *A well-planted hanging basket will be a mass of colour all summer long.*

Index

***Above:** Fruit and flowers make a charming combination, as shown with these strawberries and pelargoniums.*

Index

Above: *Herbs can be just as decorative as bedding plants, and have the advantage of being useful, too.*